"

God's Rhythm
The Key to Prosperity
For This Age

By

Greg Dalesssandri

**God's Rhythm
The Key to Prosperity for this Age**

ISBN 0-9771325-0-1

Unless otherwise indicated, all scripture quotations are taken from the King James Version of the Bible

**1st Edition June 2005
2nd Edition May 2006**

Contents

Greg Dalessandri

Here are a few comments from the students of TradingFaith.com

There is definitely a God thing working through Greg and the mentoring program. The system works period. Greg teaches you how to gain understanding of the rhythm of the market, how to find the proper trade set-ups entries, exits, how to set daily goals, and so much more. The training/mentoring is a small, very small price to pay for a developed skill you can use the rest of your life. Greg has spent many years developing and perfecting this system. I see the hand of God in this system and how the Lord has blessed Greg's commitment to training/mentoring others. The difference is, he cares and desires to see each of us fulfill our vision in life.

Greg Dalessandri

Greg has helped me personally work through many issues in my trading
Florida

I'm emailing you from Ghana Africa where we're ministering to 400 pastors and leaders....desperate situations in their churches and ministries...wow!

Hey, I've been trading online in Philippines, Africa and elsewhere...and God has been very good to me! I've totally paid for my trips through trading over the last couple of months and am so thankful for God for insight and wisdom - that you've delivered into me....
Texas

THANK YOU for sharing your trading process with the IBD Meetup group last evening. I know many of us were "blown away" with the concepts
Arizona

Greg

I would like to thank the Lord and you for your decision to help others in learning to trade. Give a man a fish and feed him for the day. Teach a man to fish and feed him for life. I appreciate your promise and your motivation which you spell out on your website for the entire world to see
Virginia

Greg,

I want you to know that I've doubled my contracts for the second straight 10 day period in a row... I promised myself if I could trade and get my 20 points in the AM for 10 days in a row, I'd double contracts. This is my 2nd time to double...and have had perfect days of trading - miraculously! Thanks Greg for your mentorship and believing in me. I'm going to continue to grow as a trader until one day where I can fund large kingdom ventures based on the first 2 hours of the market.... I'm so excited!!!
Texas

Greg

Thanks for the Video Recaps!…they are REALLY helpful. I had great fun yesterday made 4 on the S&P and 30.5 on the DOW. I seemed to know where it was ultimately going. Also, have had great support from Terranova technical support… Your help is absolutely the greatest.

Texas

Greg called me and said, "You need to check out this fib thing, it's amazing!" I said, "Ok Greg give me the numbers for tomorrow." This was on a Thursday afternoon. I didn't get to watch the market that Friday. On Saturday, I brought my wife in the office and said, "Let's see if Greg knows what he is doing." He nailed those numbers to the upside and the downside within a point. I asked him to explain the whole plan to me and I practiced it for a month without any daily losses. I went on the simulator and had the same results. My wife kept telling me to go live, but I was scared to go live. I tried for over 2 years to make it and couldn't. Well I went live and took my account and doubled it in 4 weeks. And now my dad is trading again with me. Our relationship is great now! I look back at it and see that every time I was going to quit trading, Greg would show up in my life. I know God put Greg in my life not only to help me with my trading but to be a good friend in Christ. He helps keep me on the right path. Trading is what my dad and I have in common and it allows us to have a good relationship that we might not have had without a common interest.

I thank God for everything and Greg for being there when I need him.
Arizona

Just wanted to let you know that last nights Personal Mentoring class was amazing. The discussion about focusing on the premise of your trades, both before and after you're in them, was a missing link for me. Definitely light bulb material!
Oregon

Greg,

I just wanted to let you know how impressed I have been with the personal mentoring. During one of our mentoring classes, Tom mentioned how much more he got out of the DVD's after some mentoring. I've gone back and reviewed the DVD's also, and he's right, they seem to come alive with new information. The DVD's are great, the information is all there, but without the personal mentoring I'm sure I would not have gotten as much out of them. I've read the Rich Dad series of books and he attributes his success largely to finding a mentor. I've been looking for a mentor for a while, and I have had a tough time finding someone who fits the bill in all areas. Your expertise is obvious. You have excellent skills as a teacher, and I believe you really do care about the people you are mentoring. Based on what I've seen at other sites, your service is superior, and a terrific value. While I've had some success on my own as a full time trader, I'm sure

that working with you has taken years off my learning curve, and saved me a lot of painful (expensive) mistakes that I would have made on my own. I look forward to working with you in the future.
Thanks again Greg.
Wisconsin

Hi Greg;
Got my points 5 days in a row, thank God… Minnesota

Holy Moly,
20 points in two trades today! BOOYA.
Thanks for all your help,
Oregon

Greg
My wife and I just got back from an 8 day vacation on the beaches of the Caribbean. Thanks for teaching me to get my points every day.
Arizona

Greg,
I made a place to re-watch the videos and

the last WTTCM class of 11/18 on Sunday. Can't tell you how great it was and the fun I had today in the market. Each day of my paper trading gets better and I am making my daily objectives more consistently. It works. The WTTCM's each Thursday continue to be amazing...its great. The repetition and the new ideas and challenges forever seem to be helpful. I owe a great deal to you for the mentoring and my son for getting me included in your mentoring group. Given a little time and practice, I'll be a professional trader with the income far exceeding my original objectives. Can't say much more that Thanks...couldn't have done it financially without your guidance.

Texas

Dedications

My heart has been upheld through this journey by my Lord and Savior...Jesus! His Holy Spirit has been at my right hand pointing out the direction and vision, my precious wife has been on my left, standing in faith and believing in me through all the pitfalls and naysayers, she is truly magnificent! My Love for you grows everyday! My children for their unconditional love, and who have given me insight into the heart of God! My In-laws George and Babe Moerkerke, whose financial blessings in the beginning, made all of this possible. They are truly blessed with the Gift of Giving! And my Grandfather, whose prayers, support and encouragement, through my entire life ...

You Truly Are My
"Best Man"!

And, of course the students of TradingFaith that I have had the privilege of working with, you have helped me to shape and polish the training.
Thank You!

Cover Design:
Dina Remi
www.DinaRemi.com
Dyrtist@gmail.com

Forward

This book was written to capture and express the vision that God has birthed, created and is unfolding before me. Over the last 6 years I have had countless conversations where I have had the opportunity to share this vision. The fulfillment of this vision, and the movement that is currently underway is in the very beginning stages. I believe the Body of Christ is about to move into an area of financial outpouring that the scriptures speak of. The wealth of the world is for the first time in history available and literally at our fingertips. (Proverbs 13:22) This book, in very practical terms discusses this reality, and how to seize it!

Each person that hears and responds to this vision is responding to the calling of the Holy Spirit to fund the Spreading of the Gospel, and do Good Works. The great

Commission to the Ministry of Reconciliation is at hand. It is the time for the Church to take the place and position that it should be walking and functioning in.

What a privilege and testimony to the world it will be for the Church to take on the burden that the Governments and States have had to bear.

Many that have heard this vision are telling their friends and family. They have them visit the web site that I have created to facilitate the "Training for God's Covenant People" needed for this movement, and then they encourage them to call me directly so that I can share the vision with them personally.

This book contains the truths from those conversations. I was finding myself on the phone sharing the truths and revelations you will find in the following pages, 10-20 hours a week. Writing this book is as much of a need as a joy!

The victory and fulfillment of the revelation set forth in these pages is alive and breathing, through the students of TradingFaith. It is my heart to continue to be diligent and obedient for the part that I can play in this move through TradingFaith.

I sincerely pray that the words in this book will spark a vision, burden and prayer for this movement, which God is calling to action.

Blessings on all you put your hands to, and on the seed that you sow!

Greg

Greg Dalessandri

Chapter 1

Our Fields Have Been Too Small

In this book we will be covering the five basic precepts, or building blocks that makes the title of this book "God's Rhythm" The key to Prosperity for this Age, a reality. The precepts that we will be discussing will bring you to an understanding of what I call "Practical Prosperity" We are about to embark on a journey that is so practical that at the end of this book you will know exactly what to do to become a part of the distribution of wealth that we so desperately need to bring in the necessary money to fund the Spreading of the Gospel. This movement is in the very beginning stages. The wave is just starting to build. You will come to understand that the things that were needed to be in place to facilitate this financial outpouring, have only come together, and been available in the last few years! This is a very exciting time that we live in, and God is looking for those that want to participate. Hang on, "Practical Prosperity" here we come!

The first precept I would like to spend some time on, is discussing the idea of prosperity in general. There are plenty of incredible books out there covering this subject, so it is my intent to only briefly touch on this area.

God promised Abraham that his descendants were to number as the sands of the seas (Gen. 22:17), as the Father of the Faith, God would "prosper his way" (Gen 24:40), and to Abraham's descendants, as God's "chosen people", were given the "power to get wealth; that he may establish his covenant" (Deut 8:18). All other people were Gentiles and not heirs of the covenant and the promises that God established with Abraham.

The Hebrew people have walked in this revelation ever since the covenant was established with Abraham.

So the question became, how can the Gentiles also partake of the blessings of the Abrahamic covenant. The answer is through the shed blood of the Messiah, Jesus Christ (Acts 14:27, 15:7, 28:28)

When Jesus the Christ died on the cross, and with his final words "It Is Finished" (John 19:30), the veil of the holy of holies was "rent in two", (Matt 27:51) and the new covenant was birthed. The Abrahamic covenant became the old covenant. The new covenant provided that there was no longer the differentiation of Jew and Gentile, but all who believe in the provision of forgiveness of the shed blood of the Messiah, Jesus Christ are to receive all the promises and blessings included in the old and new covenants (Gal 3:14)

I studied a teaching series by Kenneth Copeland in the mid 80's on the subject of the covenants. It was an incredible revelation of both the old and new covenants. I would highly recommend this kind of study, as I believe your life and walk with God will be intensely blessed by it.

So now all who believe in the provision of Jesus death, burial and resurrection, are under a new covenant, and walk as true sons of God and heirs of the all the promises that the old and new covenants bring with them (Rom 1:16) (Gal 3:29) (Eph 3:6)

Does this new covenant provide a purpose for the prosperity promise of the old covenant?

The new covenant tells us that the believer will live eternally as inhabitants of God's kingdom. Aside from our daily needs here, everything else is temporal in contrast to the promise of living an eternity of reigning and ruling with God and Christ in the heavenlies.

So, if we are heavenly minded, why should we be concerned with prospering at all, or that it is part of the promises included in the covenants?

Because, we are commissioned under the new covenant to bring the ministry of reconciliation to the world (2 Cor 5:18). The ministry of reconciliation means that anyone through Christ's provision can be reconciled to God! We are commissioned to further this ministry. We are commissioned to spread that Gospel or Good News! (Mark 16:15) Financial prosperity will allow us to accomplish this.

It is my opinion that this is the primary, maybe the only reason that we are to prosper.

Jesus said he would not return until the Gospel or Good News of his shed blood and the forgiveness that comes with it by belief, is spread thru "all the world" (Matt 24:14). God's heart is that none would perish but have everlasting life (Matt 18:14)(John 3:15-16).

Does this mean that those that do not believe in the Good News of Christ's Redemption do not live eternally? No, both the believer and unbeliever's soul lives on eternally. The difference is the believer gets to reside with God in his kingdom (John 3:16)(Luke 23:43). The non-believers by their own choice of not accepting Christ's Redemption do not get to reside with God and instead are to live eternally separated from him. Herein lies the problem, by choosing to be separated from God they are also choosing to be separated from his Love, Goodness, and Protection. The only other people or beings outside of God's presence are others that have rejected him.

This would also include Lucifer and 1/3 of the angels that have been banished from his presence. The 1/3 of the angels are now called demons.

Now, can you imagine a place void of God's Love, Goodness, and Protection? A place called Hell, where you are eternally separated from God in "outer darkness"? (2 Thess 1:9)(Matt 25:30) Where you have Lucifer and the demons that hate God, co-inhabiting a place with mankind, who is made in the likeness of God? Can you imagine having to live in a place with Lucifer and the demons where they have no restraints and where mankind has no protection for all eternity!

No wonder Christ called it a place of "weeping and gnashing of teeth" and the "smoke of their torment ascendeth up for ever and ever and they have no rest day or night"(Matt 8:12)(Rev 14:11).

This is exactly why God has called us to the Ministry of Reconciliation!

He made us in his image! We are his Children! He Loves us, and created us to fellowship with him! We are the apple of his eye! He wants to spend eternity with us! He wants us all to accept his salvation through Jesus and not be separated from him, his Love, Goodness, and Protection! His desire is for everyone to live forever with Him, Jesus, the Angels, the Saints of Old and with our Loved Ones in the heavenlies! He wants us to reign and rule with him! What a future! He wants everyone to know this! "Spread the Gospel" or "Good News" is his Heart, and now Our Commission!

Again, It is my position, that this is the primary reason that God wants us to prosper. To fund and participate in Spreading the Gospel of Good News!

So again, does God want us to prosper so that we can fund the Spreading of the Gospel?

YES!

But why stop at the ministry of reconciliation only. How about the Church having the funding to take its true position of doing "Good Works"? (Eph 2:10)(2Cor 9:7-8) What a privilege and honor for the Church to step up and take on the role and burden that the Government and State have been bearing. It truly is the Church's position to take on that burden. Caring for the widows, orphans and the sick and needy. Can you imagine the "Good Works" the church can do if we were prospering! (Prov 13:22)

God is using the Holy Spirit and the Scriptures to speak to the hearts of believers to this ministry. By this prompting believers have sought out how to raise the funds to support the spreading of the gospel.

When I first became a Christian in February 1981, I remember the word being preached and taught concerning the prosperity of the church and the blessing that would come from the financial outpouring. I received that word, I was on board, sign me up, I want to be a blessing, a giver, God count on me, was my heart.

What we were missing was the law of seed and harvest. As we have grown to understand the seed/ harvest principle, we have realized that the amount of our harvest is in direct proportion to the amount of our sowing. (Gal 6:7) God watches over his word to fulfill it. Ok God, to be a giver, to be a blessing, to be part of those that prosper and fund the ministry of reconciliation you need us to sow seed! WOW, I want to sow, I have some seed, I will not eat my seed, I will plant it, and as it dies it will bear much fruit (John 12:24)

Now I need to talk and expound on the concept of our fields being too small.

If you have a whole barn full of seed but only an acre to plant in, your harvest is only going to be as big as your field.

Greg Dalessandri

If you open a pizza shop, you are limited in how many pizzas you can make.
How many people you can seat, how many phone lines you can answer and how many delivery people you can have delivering.

As believers we understand that we are God's people, and that we are to prosper to fulfill the ministry of reconciliation. However, the fields that we have had to plant into, to receive our harvest have simply been too small.

Soon after I become a believer, I began attending Christian Businessmen's meetings. They were great! We would hear their testimonies and vision, and how God was moving in their business's to bring fulfillment to the prosperity that we knew and believed God for. I can remember discussing the idea that Christian Business's would fulfill the vision and fund the gospel. This worked to some degree, but the size of the field that the seed was going into was too small. How many have the resources or the time to start a business? The number of individuals that have the resources and the time that can endeavor into a profitable business is limited.

Next came the Multi Level Marketing (MLM) opportunities like Amway etc. This allowed the average person with limited resources to start their own business, and start to take part in receiving and distributing the prosperity to further the ministry of reconciliation. There were problems here also, the fields had built in limitations, and were too small.

The main thing to understand here is that most people have limits to the resources and time they have to dedicate to this purpose and vision. And even given the time and resources, the fields still can not produce the kind of prosperity harvest that is needed to not only fulfill the ministry of reconciliation, but also to fund the church to do Good Works and take its true position.

Now comes the amazing thing. Drum roll please…what if I told you that we are right now, for the first time in history, living in an age where all the world's wealth is available, at our very fingertips! No limits on the size of the field! None! The field size is now unlimited! Again, the field size is now unlimited! And, where the problem of peoples limited resources and time are completely minimized! (Prov 13:22)

The Financial Markets are the answer! We are now able to live the reality of "Practical Prosperity" and Receive the Funds to Spread the Gospel and Do Good Works!

This is what this book is dedicated to. With a broad stroke to bring to light the reality of the fulfillment of God's heart, that we would have the funds necessary to spread the Gospel to the ends of the earth, and for the church to do Good Works and take its true position.

Through the rest of this book I will be bringing to light some very powerful concepts of how this term "Practical Prosperity" is alive and real.

Before we go any further I want to say this one thing. You do not have to have a lot of money to make this a reality as you may be thinking. I will go into much more detail in the following chapters on this truth, but for now understand this, with an account size of $2,500 to $10,000, I will show you how to make from as little as $24,000 to over 1 million in one year, all in a just a few hours a day. Simply put, Chapter 3 is going to "Knock your Socks Off"

I know you are thinking NO WAY. That's ok, that's why I am writing this book. Commit to finish reading these pages and you will see that I will lay out the realities of this truth without question.

The Financial Market holds the answer, and believers simply do not know this.

Greg Dalessandri

"Where there is no vision, the people perish" (Prov 29:18), or in this case both vision and understanding.

There are three basic ways to gather wealth. Owning a Business, Real Estate, and the Financial Markets. The misunderstandings, simple ignorance and timing of technology advancements concerning the financial markets has kept believers from receiving the funds that we need and are now simply sitting there.

The Body of Christ needs to be ready to fulfill the ministry of reconciliation to the world by accepting the Resources or Money required.

Since 1999 God has been guiding me through the truths that you will find in the following pages. God met me along the journey at every step. In the very beginning, I promised God that once he taught me how to be a Trader that I would be willing to teach anyone that he sent to me.

This book and everything that I have done to create a training organization dedicated to training the Body of Christ to become "Traders for the Master", I have done to be obedient to that promise.

I am truly committed to this cause, and believe that this truly is the first time in history that the wealth of the world is literally right at our fingertips.

I was asked to write this book and share this vision back in 2003. I felt that I should not do this until the truths in this book were more then just a vision, but truly a reality

As you will see as we proceed, this is now true, and the vision has become a reality.

This book is dedicated to not just share the vision and get you excited, but also to give you the practical steps necessary so you can take part in this financial outpouring if you are being called to participate.

It was these practical steps and specifically the training/ mentoring that had to be in place, fully functioning and successful before I could write this book.

From 1999, I spent the first four years in a long, expensive, exhausting learning process. Thru that process I discovered that the strategies that were being taught to traders, were simply not working very well.

After the first three years God revealed to me "Leveraged Instruments" or "What to Trade". This was a huge precept building block. That revelation is what makes the money possibilities that I was referring to a bit ago possible. It is also the revelation that makes it possible for those with smaller accounts to participate as well, so anyone in the Body of Christ that is called to this financial outpouring can participate! We will cover this precept further in chapter 3.

After receiving the revelation of "What to Trade", I had the freedom and focus to be in a position to receive the next revelation of "God's Rhythm" or "How to Trade". This was the next critical building block that I needed to understand, and is beyond a shadow of doubt, a very powerful yet simple concept. I have seen Professional Traders, Brokers, Money Managers, Investment Clubs and people from every walk of life stand completely in awe as I have presented this incredible revelation.

Greg Dalessandri

It doesn't do you much good to know "What to Trade" if you do not know "How to Trade"

This building block of "God's Rhythm" is absolutely critical to walking in "Practical Prosperity". It is what gives the understanding and insight into the Financial Markets movements and puts the trader in a position to predict these movements before they happen with incredible reliability. It is this precept that makes it possible for anyone to become a "Trader for the Master", achieving the financial objectives to fund the Spreading of the Gospel that we have been discussing. We will be covering this further in chapter 4.

After I received these revelations, people responded and started asking me to train them to be "Traders for the Master". I could see that the students needed much more than I was able to give them at that time. So, I started to envision and create the necessary training tools that they would need.

It soon became my heart to develop a full training organization dedicated to the Body of Christ that could develop "Traders for the Master".

NOW with God's help that organization has been created.

Because this has been created and is fully functioning, the vision is now more then just a vision, but in fact has become a fulfillment of the vision, and this book can now shout this practical message.

TradingFaith.com was started in the summer of 2004. The quality, and content is creating "Traders for the Master" everyday that are walking in "Practical Prosperity" and are training to function in

Greg Dalessandri

the role of dispersing funds for the Spreading of the Gospel and to do Good Works.

The training organization includes a complete mentoring program and is designed to bring a novice to the level of being a "Trader for the Master" in a few months. I will discuss this powerful training process further in chapter 5, "Training for God's Covenant People".

So to summarize: In this chapter we have discussed the covenants, why prosper, our commission to the ministry of reconciliation and the concept that "Our Fields Have Been Too Small". We have also discovered that the Financial Market is a place where we can seize the wealth required to do Good Works and Fund the Spreading of the Gospel to the ends of the Earth. And, that for the first time in history this wealth is literally at our fingertips.

In the rest of this book, I will set out to discuss the four additional precepts that will bring further clarity to the concept of "Practical Prosperity". Join me, as we will next discuss:

- "The Technology Age"

- "Leveraged Instruments" or …
  "What to Trade"

- "God's Rhythm" or …
  "How to Trade"

- And Practical Training designed for…
  "God's Covenant People"

Chapter 2

The Technology Age

The first thing that was necessary in making "Practical Prosperity" a reality is the Technology Age. One of the first things that occurred that prepared the way for the technology advancements that were to come, was a ruling in 1975 where commissions on trades were deregulated. This set the stage for lower cost Discount Brokerages to emerge. Up until then Full Service Brokerages was the only option. The emergence of the Discount Brokerages made it much more affordable to execute trades.

This paved the way for the Direct Access Brokers, which gave even more affordable trades with the added feature of extremely fast execution speeds. With the advent of the broadband high-speed Internet connections, these executions could be as fast as seconds…or even faster! In 1999 I was one of the first homes in the northern part of Phoenix to have a cable high-speed or broadband Internet connection. I was able to connect to the Markets through my direct access high-speed connection and execute trades in seconds at minimal costs per trade. It took another couple of years for my computer to catch up to the demands of the amount of data that I was watching. My computer upgrade to a Windows XP, 3.0 Intel CPU chip with 2 gig of ram memory, is doing a great job keeping up with the data I am receiving and need to watch from the financial markets, on my LCD monitors.

You see, up until just a few short years ago none of this was possible.

The Technology Age has made the wealth of the world available and literally at our fingertips.

Incredibly fast and affordable trade executions enabled by the Direct Access Broker, and the high-speed Internet connection combined with the power of the newer computers and with multiple monitors to watch it all…was the first critical building block and key to unlocking the wealth God has for us!

Let me further discuss and clarify the role of the Broker. In order to trade you have to have an account with a broker. A Full Service or Discount Broker takes your order and takes the necessary steps to get your order filled for you. They can go out and satisfy your order through another broker, an individual or from their own supply. It doesn't really matter where they get the supply to satisfy your order. The important piece to understand here is that they execute or manage your order/ trade for you.

The Direct Access Broker takes a "hands off" approach. This means that you manage your own trade directly (have direct access) to the other institutions participating or wanting to trade. The Direct Access Broker simply receives a commission every time you trade.

The execution speed is the main difference and the reason that this is a discussion point. To be an active trader, execution or the speed that you can be filled on a trade is critical. So opening an account with a Direct Access Broker is the recommended direction. The amount of money needed to open the account is specific to each broker and based on what you want to trade. We will discuss this further in the next chapter.

The next thing to understand is that each broker not only holds your money, but also provides some type of software for you to actually execute a trade. There are features that are crucial and that need to be in the software. Besides features like; full charting and execution capabilities, you also want to be able to "play trade" with fake money during the learning startup process. You typically do this in a demo or simulator mode. The broker that we use and recommend and the software that they supply are best of their class and offer these features. We will discuss our recommended Direct Access Broker and the Software they supply further in the final chapter.

The main purpose for this chapter is to bring to your understanding how we are truly in a brand new AGE. The decisions by the financial markets governing bodies, along with the advancements of technology have set the stage for us to reach out and seize the wealth of the world!

Now that the wealth of the world has been brought right to our fingertips, how do we actually go get it? We will now continue on our journey to discuss these very things!

Greg Dalessandri

Chapter 3

Leveraged Instruments What To Trade

The Financial Markets hold the answer to "Practical Prosperity". We need to have a quick discussion on what the Markets actually are.

There are really multiple markets. Picture if you will a fish market, a vegetable market, and a fruit market etc. The Financial Markets are basically organized the same way. The different markets where stocks and or instruments are traded are called "Exchanges". Each of these exchanges trade different instruments. Or, different instruments are traded on each exchange. The most widely known of all the exchanges is the New York Stock Exchange (NYSE). Can you guess what is traded on that exchange...Stocks.

The Nasdaq, is another exchange where stocks are traded and the two exchanges compete for companies to list their stock on their exchange. If you want to buy/ sell or trade Microsoft's stock you would have to go to the Nasdaq exchange to accomplish this. Microsoft stock is traded on the Nasdaq exchange under the ticker symbol MSFT. If you want to trade Home Depot's stock you would have to go to the NYSE to trade that stock. It is traded under the ticker symbol HD.

There are a number of other exchanges where other instruments are traded. For example Oil and Gas are traded on the New York Mercantile Exchange or the NYMEX. Options are traded on the Chicago Board of Options Exchange or the CBOE. Commodities and Futures are traded on the Chicago Mercantile Exchange, or the CME.

Most countries also have exchanges. The Japanese Exchange is called the Nikkei, the German Exchange, the DAX and so on.

Because of technology access via the Internet, and coordination by the brokers, the barriers between the exchanges have been eliminated here in the US. So as a trader you have access through your Broker to any of the exchanges that you want, and can trade the instruments in each exchange as you desire. Each Broker may have limitations to what you can trade based on their licensing, and each exchange has its own rules that need to be considered beyond what instruments are traded on their exchange. But for now, if you understand that there are multiple exchanges and that different instruments are traded on each exchange, and that you can trade on any of the exchanges seamlessly through the software provided by your Broker, then you have the understanding needed to proceed.

As the markets matured there arose the need to get a feel or "Gauge" of how the markets are performing for the day, week, month etc. You could always go look at your individual stock or instrument, but what about the birds eye view across the entire market? The markets responded by creating the gauges called Market Indexes. The Dow, S&P 500, and NASDAQ are three of these types of gauges that tell us how the markets are performing.

Lets first discuss the Major Market Index called the DOW. The DOW Index is comprised of 30 Stocks. They are sometimes referred to as the Blue Chips. The DOW is nothing more then an average of how all 30 of the stocks that comprise the DOW performed for the day, week, month etc...averaged. The DOW like the S&P500 and the NASDAQ are called Indexes for this very reason. They are simply an index of how the markets are performing. The DOW: the top 30 stocks. The S&P500: the top 500 stocks etc.

Are the 30 stocks that comprise the DOW also potentially included in the S&P 500

Index? …Yes. There isn't any formal rule that says that if a stock is in one Index it cannot be in another. The Indexes are simply a measurement of how the broader markets are performing, and therefore can be any grouping. Many Institutions and full Service Brokers create their own Indexes, made up of the stocks they feel give a better representation of the markets broader or overall performance. The board that make the decisions of what goes into each Major Market Index reviews the contents periodically and sometimes makes decisions to rebalance the index. For example, AT&T was dropped from the DOW and another stock was chosen to replace it.

The next step in understanding "Practical Prosperity" includes the concept that we will only be trading the Major Market Indexes. Not any of the individual stocks that comprise the Indexes, but the Indexes themselves.

How can we trade an Index you ask? Isn't it just a gauge of how the markets are performing? Remember, there are multiple exchanges and each offer or provide instruments that are traded.

The American Exchange or AMEX offers an instrument that mirrors the Major Market Indexes. If you want to be immediately diversified across all the 30 stocks that comprise the DOW, you can trade this one instrument called the Diamonds. The ticker symbol is DIA. By trading the DIA on the AMEX exchange you are essentially trading the entire group of 30 stocks at once. Does the AMEX also have a instrument that mirrors the S&P 500? Yes, it is called the Spyders and the symbol is SPY.

How popular are these stock instruments that basically are the entire Market Index as opposed to trading the individual stocks? Huge…Enormous! The trading world has embraced these instruments as a very popular way of trading.

The daily trading volume on the SPY is greater then some of the widest traded individual stocks on the market.

You are essentially trading the broader Market, you are immediately diversified across the broader market. It is stable, solid, not normally subject to the swings that an individual stock can be subject too etc. Trading the Market Indexes is much safer then trading individual stocks. The symbol's SPY and DIA are considered Market Index...Stocks. So they are actually traded, recognized and treated as a stock, even though they represent an index or a broader group of stocks.

Based on all this information, I focus on, and train our traders to only trade the Major Markets Indexes only. We are not chasing individual stocks, or the hot stock of the day type thing.

This focus is what enabled God to help me to understand and learn the precepts that we will discuss in the next chapter "God's

Rhythm" or "How to Trade". You see most traders spend more time trying to find "What to Trade" and that leaves little time or energy left to then learn "How to Trade". The amount of homework and study dedicated to finding the stocks that the trader wants to trade can be enormous. This is just one of the reasons that a majority of traders struggle and fail. I eliminate that wasted energy by focusing the trader on the broader market i.e., the solid, stable, DOW and S&P500.

I have just introduced you to the Major Market Index Stocks, i.e. the SPY and the DIA. However, we are not done, we will **not be** trading the SPY or DIA Index Stocks. There is something even better!

I now must introduce a concept called Leverage.

Leverage is basically this; the concept that you can **Do Much with Little.**

Leverage or "Leveraged Instruments" is the next critical precept and building block that makes "Practical Prosperity" a reality. This revelation that I received back in 2002, is what has made it possible for those with what has been considered a relatively small account (under $10,000) to take part in this move of financial outpouring, to collect funds for the purpose of fulfilling the great commission!

Let me say that again. Those with relatively small accounts can now be part of this financial outpouring to further the Ministry of Reconciliation!

The amount of money needed to open and effectively trade a Leveraged Account is much…much smaller then a normal or typical stock trading account. Hold on here we go! You are about to see how this works!

As we have mentioned, from now on we will only be focused on and trading the Major Market Indexes. Which includes the DOW, and the S&P500. Not individual stocks like Microsoft, Intel, Citibank, Johnson & Johnson etc.

Just the solid, stable, Major Market Indexes. We trade the entire DOW Not the individual stocks that comprise the DOW.

You can trade the entire group of 30 stocks in the DOW a few different ways. We have already discussed that you can trade the entire 30 stocks in the DOW, in one trade, by trading the Diamonds or DIA on the AMEX.

The other way that you can trade the entire 30 stocks in the DOW is by trading the Major Market Index Futures Contract on the CBOT exchange. The symbol is YM. This type of Futures Contract is also called an Emini.

The DIA and the YM are basically the same. They both mirror the movement of the DOW Major Index, which is comprised of the 30 stocks that make up the DOW Index. They both have all the benefits of the Major Market Index that we have already discussed, but here is how they differ.

The DIA is traded on the AMEX and is recognized, treated and traded as an index **STOCK**.

The YM is traded on the CBOT as a Futures Contract and is recognized, treated and traded as an Index **FUTURES CONTRACT**, and as a futures contract it is treated differently then a stock.

So same movement but treated differently…how you ask?

In a number of ways, for now we will discuss the most prominent way that they differ…**COST!**

Here is where the Leverage comes in!!

The cost of 1 share of the DIA is $100 (rounding based on the DOW being at 10000).

500 shares of the DIA will cost you $50,000 ($100 x 500).

The cost of 1 contract of the YM is currently $1,250.

1 contract of the YM is equal to 500 shares of the DIA

So a $1,250 purchase cost of the YM Emini is equal to the $50,000 purchase cost of the DIA stock.

They both mirror the movement of the DOW Index throughout the day. They both pay the exact same profit and loss with the same movement, But with a huge difference in what you have to pay for it.

The current average daily movement on the DOW is currently 60-90 points a day. This is the net movement at the end of the day, not the true amount of movement that occurs during the day. For example, the nightly news report at the end of the day reflecting a +50 point day for the DOW does not reflect the actual amount of movement for the day. It just finished +50 at the close of the trading day from the previous day's closing price. It is not uncommon to have 150+ point movement during the day. Up and Down all around thing.

The goal of the traders that I work with in the TradingFaith mentoring program is to capture 10-20 points of the DOW's movement a day. This goal is what I call our "Manna for the Day".

With a 20-point move of the DOW, trading either the DIA stock or the YM Emini, a trader will be paid $100. The trader will make the same $100 regardless of which instrument he trades, the YM

Emini Index Futures Contract or the DIA Index Stock.

The trader will make the same $100 on the $1,250 YM investment or the $50,000 DIA investment.

The YM trader made an 8% return on their $1,250 investment in 1 day.
The DIA trader just made a .02% return on their $50,000 investment in 1 day.

Same return, tons less money! That's what we call Leverage!

Now you can see why, once I received this revelation, I realized that the entire Body of Christ could walk in this! The old truth that the market was only for the wealthy is not true any longer! Anyone with a relatively small bag of seed can produce huge quantities of harvest. And as the bag of seed grows, as we will soon see, will allow the trader to produce a harvest that is truly remarkable. This is due the concept that the field size is basically unlimited.

Again, in our example the trader made $100 on a $1,250 investment! Again, that's an 8% return in 1 DAY! It is our trader's goal to capture their "Manna for the Day" of 10-20 points a day.

Now, lets look at two scenarios; an account that is under $10,000 and one that is above $10,000. We will only be trading the YM Dow Emini Index Futures Contract since we just discovered that trading the DIA Index Stock couldn't compare to the % return and account size reality of trading the YM Dow Emini.

The broker that we recommend (we will discuss this broker in more detail later) requires at least $5,000 to open an account. But once opened you just need to maintain enough in the account to trade.

With an account under $10,000 the cost of the YM contract increases to $2,500.

So someone with a $2,500 account can trade 1 contract. Capturing 20 points a day is a 4% return and will pay $100 a day or $2,000 a month. That's $24,000 a year!

A $5,000 account capturing the same 20 points a day would again be a 4% return and will pay $200 a day or $4000 a month. That's $48,000 a year!

And in both cases the original principal of $2,500 and $5,000 is still there!

Now, lets look at the results based on a $15,000 account. With an account over $10,000 each contract costs $1,250. With a $15,000 account I can trade 12 contracts in one trade. By trading a $15,000 account capturing 20 points a day, I would receive an 8% return and $1,200 in 1 DAY!!! Or, $24,000 a Month!

That's 288,000 a year!!!
And again the original principal of
$15,000 is still there!

With a $30,000 account...
$576,000 A Year
With a $60,000 account...
$1,152,000 A Year
And on, And on!

Now in this example we are leaving the $15,000 original principal in the account in place as seed. The trader is withdrawing the profits I call this, the "Cash Flow" model example.

IF, YOU LEAVE THE PROFITS IN THE ACCOUNT AND ALLOW IT TO GROW SO YOU CAN TRADE THE TOTAL AMOUNT OF CONTRACTS THAT THE ACCOUNT WILL ALLOW YOU TO BUY.... THE RESULTS ARE SIMPLY STAGGERING!!!!

Let's take a closer look at this scenario where we leave the profits in, and "Compound" the account. We will be capturing 20 points a day, however, with this scenario you leave the profits in the account and you trade as many contracts that the account can afford. In this "Compounding" model you are basically allowing your account to grow, as opposed to our previous "Cash Flow" model example.

We will start with $10,000 in our trading account for this example, and we will be capturing 20 points a day …

You will have over 4 Million in Real Cash in ONE YEAR! [1]

This "Compounding" model example includes all trading costs and allows the trader to capture their 20 points in 10 trades a day, or 50 trades to capture 100 points a week.

Every day that the trader uses fewer trades to capture their points, the leftover trades rollover to another day. The better you are as a trader, meaning the less trades it takes to capture the 20 points a day the better… and accelerates the results!

The problem here is that it would be difficult for most traders to let the account grow for an entire year without drawing any funds out for living expenses etc. Ok, in this "Compounding" model example,

I have also included a $500 daily draw after the first 2 months!

The Trading System, which we will discuss in the next chapter "God's Rhythm" "How to Trade" and the "Training for God's Covenant People" that we will discuss in chapter 5, fine-tunes the traders to capture their daily point goals each day.

Are you intrigued yet? … There is more!

NOW LET'S CONSIDER SOMEONE WHO WOULD LIKE TO TRADE FOR OTHERS

Would most investors be happy with a money manager that produced 100% returns a year? (Matthew 25:15)

Of Course!

Lets say that 100 people give you $10,000 each to manage/ trade on their behalf. This one million dollar account would allow you to buy 500 contracts of the ES's. The ES S&P500 Emini contract would work best for this size of an account. Let's figure out how many points a **month** you would have to capture trading 500 contracts to get a **100% Annual Return.**

The answer...
5 Points A Month!

That's a 100% Return a Year!

Remember our training is designed to teach the traders to capture their "Manna for the Day", or **10-20** points a **DAY** trading the Ym's. This would equate to **1-2** points a **DAY** trading the ES S&P Emini contract.

5 points a **MONTH** would produce a **100%** return a **YEAR!**

In this example, trading costs are included and we are NOT Compounding, we are trading the 500 contracts that our original principal in the account allowed. We did not increase the number of contracts based on the increased value of the fund each month!

And, considering the volume of contracts that you are trading, you can possibly negotiate discounts on commissions, which could reduce your trading costs!

Are you starting to understand why this precept is so important to walking in "Practical Prosperity"? By trading the Emini's "Leveraged Instruments" the door is open to basically anyone that feels the call to respond to this financial outpouring and become a "Trader for the Master".

I would like to take a moment at this time to discuss the type of percentages that we have been looking at in light of God's harvest economy.

Lets review the trading results with the account sizes below with the "Cash Flow" model:

$2,500 x 20 pts a day = $24,000 a year
$5,000 x 20 pts a day= $48,000 a year
$15,000 x 20 pts a day=$288,000 a year
$30,000 x 20 pts a day= $576,000 a year
$60,000 x 20 pts a day= $1,152,000 a year

The $2,500 and $5,000 accounts each produce a 1000% return.

Greg Dalessandri

The $15,000, $30,000 and $60,000 accounts each produce a 1900% return.

How do these type of returns relate to God's harvest economy?

In Matthew 13:8 Jesus said "But others (seed) fell into good ground, and brought forth fruit, some an hundredfold, some sixtyfold, some thirtyfold."

Let's consider the annual % return that we have been looking at, compared to Jesus's harvest economy of 30, 60 and 100-fold.

Using our "Cash Flow" model with a $15,000 account producing fruit of $288,000 a year is a 19-fold or a 1900% return.

We would need to produce $450,000 with our $15,000 account to receive a 30-fold or a 3000% return harvest.

We would need to produce $900,000 with our $15,000 account to receive a 60-fold or a 6000% return harvest. We would need to produce $1.5 million with our $15,000 account to receive a 100-fold or 10,000% return harvest.

As you can see, by capturing 20 points a day with a $15,000 account producing $288,000, we are only at 19-fold or a 1900% annual return.

So how can we attain the harvest returns that Jesus described? How can we turn our $15,000 account to the $450,000 30-fold, or $900,000 60-fold, or $1.5 million 100-fold harvest returns?

We could attempt to capture additional points each day using the "Cash Flow" model, or, by using the "Compounding" model (leaving the profits in the account) as we looked at in our previous example (Page 64), we can achieve the 30, 60, and 100-fold harvest that Jesus speaks of.

Isaac received a 100-fold Harvest!
(Genesis 26:12)

As we discussed in the "Compounding" example, a $10,000 account capturing 20 points with 10 trades in a day (factoring in trading costs) would produce over **4 Million in ONE YEAR**[1]...

This is actually a 400-fold or 40,000% annual return!

Trading the Eminis allows a trader to be an accomplished successful trader with a relatively small account. The money that can be achieved by trading the Emini's will certainly accomplish our commission, as I have shown you through the examples. It is also stable and diversified due to the fact that it is the Major Market Index. You also get the added benefit of being able to focus on the entire Market, not chasing individual stocks.

Now that we have settled the issue of "What to Trade", we can now embrace the next critical building block and obstacle to most traders, which is "How to Trade".

The fact that most traders spend the majority of their time trying to find "What to Trade" they are left with little time to learn "How to Trade", and therefore struggle and fail. Even if a trader learned that he could trade the Eminis without knowing the "How to Trade" concepts that we will address, can leave the trader penniless.

It doesn't do you much good to know that you can focus and trade the Eminis leveraged instruments if you do not know "How to Trade" them. We will be discussing the next critical building block and precept "God's Rhythm" or "How to Trade" in the next chapter.

This is where we will find some real breakthrough & give God the Glory!

Before we do that, if the reasons that we have already discussed are not enough, there are additional benefits to trading the

Eminis Major Market Index Future Contracts for us to understand.

The CME and CBOT exchanges offer one of, if not the fairest trading environment available to a trader! They trade overnight, so except for the weekend or a few blocks of time after the NYSE closes when they are shutdown to do system maintenance etc., they are trading and open. This means that you can set protective stops and profit targets overnight. No Overnight Gaps. This is a tremendous benefit over trading individual stocks. Also, this means that with an Internet connection they can be traded anywhere in the world! No geographical limitations. The trading volume or "liquidity" on the Eminis index futures is incredibly huge. It is an extremely popular instrument to trade. The amount of trades and contracts on the S&P Eminis a day is truly remarkable. Getting your trade executed is never a problem. Then there is the no active trader Rule. Which means that you can trade actively, or be an active trader without having a minimum of a $25,000 account. This rule applies to stocks…not Eminis index futures! There is also no Uptick Rule, which applies to shorting. There are also better taxation rules that apply to Futures. The current tax rules allow that the first 60% of profit will only be taxed at long-term capital gains rates. The current Tax Rate (2006) for long-term capital gains is 15%. Of course, some of these things could change. You should check with a CPA and your Broker on all these issues. These are just a few of the additional benefits of trading the Emini Index Futures Contracts. The Eminis truly are an incredible instrument to trade!

To summarize; we trade the entire markets with one trade. The entire market is defined as the Major Market Indexes. We trade the Dow and the S&P as our primary instruments. We trade the Major Market Indexes by trading the Eminis on the CME and CBOT exchanges. The symbol for the DOW Emini Index Future is YM and traded on the CBOT. The symbol for the

S&P500 Emini Index Future is ES and traded on the CME.

If God is calling his people to walk in financial prosperity to fund the spreading of the gospel, then the stability, leverage and account size realities afforded by the Eminis Index Futures Contracts is incredible and the revelation that the church has been looking for.

Can you believe that it is God's desire to enable believers to bring in millions in consistent cash flow to fund the Spreading of the Gospel?

Like a Flowing River!
What a Revelation!

You see that the Eminis "Leveraged Instruments" along with the "Technology Age" have paved the way

for the Body of Christ to fulfill the commission to the Ministry of Reconciliation! The Wealth is available and simply at our fingertips.

Before we can seize it though, we need to embrace and understand "God's Rhythm" or "How to Trade". It is so absolutely critical to the trader's success. It is this critical precept that will allow the trader to capture their "Manna for the Day" of 10-20 points!

After we discuss this all so important precept and building block revelation in the next chapter, we will be left with only one additional issue. That is, where does the believer called to this financial outpouring go to receive training and mentoring to walk in "Practical Prosperity" as a "Trader for the Master"?

Greg Dalessandri

1. For the purpose of the "Compounding" model example, the maximum number of contracts to be traded regardless of the size of the actual account was set at 1000 contracts. Based on current trading volume on the YM Dow Emini contract, getting an order filled of that size would be difficult. So a shift to trade the ES S&P Emini contract is factored into the calculations when the account reaches the ability to trade 50 contracts. The volume on the ES Emini contract can handle the increased size of contracts up to a 1000 contract size order and the maximum number of contract size limit for our "Compounding" model example.

Chapter 4

God's Rhythm How To Trade

"God's Rhythm", what is it, where is it, how does it work, and how does it apply to the financial markets? Specifically the Major Market Indexes and Eminis, is what we will now look at.

In my trading career after receiving the revelation of "Leveraged Instruments", I was able to focus on the Eminis. It was then that I received this next revelation of "God's Rhythm". It is this revelation that makes the capturing of "Manna for the Day", of 10-20 points with all the wealth possibilities that we discussed in the last chapter a reality! Hang on, here we go!

What is "God's Rhythm"? God introduced us to his Rhythm in the book of Genesis, in the story of creation. He wove it into the very fabric of creation. In day and night, so many hours of Day, then so many hours of Night, and also in the six days of creation, and then one day of rest.

Six days of creation, one day of rest. Rest…why did God rest? Did he need to? Was the day of rest more than the observance of the Sabbath day where we remember the Lord our God, creator of the heavens and the earth? God also created day and night and man also rested. Night wasn't to be observed as the Sabbath was. Is there more here? Was God giving us the first dynamic piece of the principles that he wove into the very fabric of his creation? Was God in essence giving us the first chapter of his manual for creation? I believe that God was revealing to us the law of what I will call "Move and Rest" or even better "God's Rhythm". Man enjoys the day, then rests.

God established a pattern or rhythm of all things, through this law of "God's Rhythm". In fact, isn't it in everything around us? Don't we know that if we do not have balance in our life, things get all out of sync. If we 'burn the candle at both ends" or "overdo it" then we will get sick. It's our body's way of reacting to not being in sync with the law of "God's Rhythm". How do we to fix our bodies? We get some rest. Understanding "God's Rhythm", the first chapter in God's manual of creation includes healthy normal rest…it is a crucial part of life in general.

There is much more to be discovered in the scriptures concerning this rhythm of "Move and Rest" or "God's Rhythm". I am confident that those gifted as teachers, will further discover and expound on this for the building of the Body of Christ. However, for our discussion concerning "Practical Prosperity", I will press on.

If this law of "God's Rhythm" is also reflected in the financial markets, how do we see, and recognize it. The first thing we need to do is find some practical way of identifying and measuring it.

I would like to now introduce you to a gentleman by the name of Leonardo Fibonacci da Pisa. He was born in Italy around 1170 AD. He was a mathematician and is credited with a number of accomplishments including defining the current number system that we use in the west.

He saw a relationship between numbers and after refining his discovery, was said to have traveled to Egypt where he saw that the pyramids reflected his newly found discoveries. He and others that have followed his work went on to find that his discoveries are reflected in the fields of art, architecture, geometry, mathematics, music, nature and in our very DNA. Everything from the way a plant grows, athletes perform, to the expansion of the universe can be understood and measured by the numbers and the relationships that Mr. Fibonacci discovered. We will discuss his finding in the generalist of terms with a focus on how his discovery brings light and understanding to the Rhythm that God wove into creation, and how it applies to "Practical Prosperity" & "How to Trade". We are looking for a way to quantify the law of "God's Rhythm" in the financial markets. Here is what he discovered.

$$0+1=1$$
$$1+1=2$$
$$1+2=3$$
$$2+3=5$$
$$3+5=8$$
$$5+8=13$$
$$8+13=21$$
$$13+21=34$$
$$21+34=55$$
$$34+55=89 \text{ and so on.}$$

What he found is that by adding the last two numbers in sequence he would come up with a series of numbers,

1,2,3,5,8,13,21,34, 55, 89 and so on. Upon further reflection and study he discovered that these numbers have a unique relationship one to another.

What he discovered is that the relationship between the numbers is 1.6 and .61. This number and relationship has been given the title of the "Golden Ratio" and is the basis for us understanding the law of "Move and Rest". It is this relationship that defines, and quantifies "God's Rhythm". I find this fact interesting; by dividing the 24 hours of the 7th day of rest into the 144 hours from the 6 remaining days of creation…you will get the value of .16.

The Golden Ratio number and relationship is also reflected in the nature of how people move and react. This includes groups of people and specifically the financial markets movement as well.

For those inclined there is a much more available on Fibonacci numbers and the "Golden Ratio" number. We will only take his study to one additional step.

This step is necessary in quantifying and measuring how the markets move and help us to understand "God's Rhythm".

We will refer to Mr. Fibonacci and his remarkable discovery as Fibs from here on out.

By looking at Fib numbers there is a truth that comes from the Golden Ratio relationship. This truth puts an actual set of calculable % numbers to the law of "Move & Rest" or "God's Rhythm". This set of calculable % numbers works like this; for every segment of movement we should rest or retrace to these levels; 24%, 38%, & 50%. The retrace can also go to the inverse of 24%, or 76% and inverse of 38% or 62%. The three that standout with the most regularity is 38%, 50% and 62%.

So for every segment of movement we should see a 38%, 50% or 62% rest or retracement move.

So what we have found is that Fibs measures or quantifies the law that God wove into creation. We can now recognize, see and react to God's law of "Move and Rest" or "God's Rhythm".

So according to Fibs a move from 0 to 100 should rest or retrace to 60, 50 or 40 before making its next move. So the Fibs give us a calculable resting period. We can also call it a reaction move. So if we get a move or leg up, we should get a reaction move or leg back to a Fib retracement level.

We see this type of display most recognizably in a mountain range.

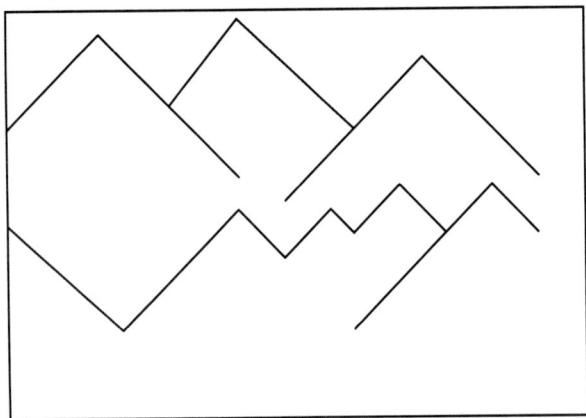

Greg Dalessandri

The farther away from the mountains, the less detail we see. As we get closer we see more detail and the number of legs and retracements increase or multiply, without losing the overall rhythm.

Mountain Ranges interestingly enough gives us one of the best representations of how the financial markets display their price movements.

As the trades are occurring during a trading period of time, we see these leg and retracement formations occurring over and over again. This display of price movement or trading activity is how we see "God's Rhythm" in a practical way and which allows us to see and predict what the market is doing as it follows "God's Rhythm".

Because this rhythm repeats itself over and over again, from the closest or "microscopic" analysis to the widest "birds eye view" analysis, we can now follow "God's Rhythm" in the financial markets with amazing results and predictability.

Is this rhythm also reflected in the Emini price/ trading movement?

YES...with the same amazing predictability!

It is this dynamics of "God's Rhythm" that teaches us how to recognize and react to price movement, specifically for our use in trading the Emini's.

It is the understanding and recognition of this rhythm that allows us to capture our "Manna for the Day"!

We will now look at an example to help you visualize and understand the law of "God's Rhythm".

We will examine an example where we get a move or leg up.

We will call the beginning of the leg "A" and the end of the leg "B".

Let's say that the beginning of the leg or point A is 250 and the top of our Leg or point B is 1550. From point A to point B the total move or leg up is 1300 pts.

Based on our understanding of Fibs we should get a rest or reaction leg back to one of the .38 .50 or .62 % retracement levels from the top of the leg or the point B at 1550.

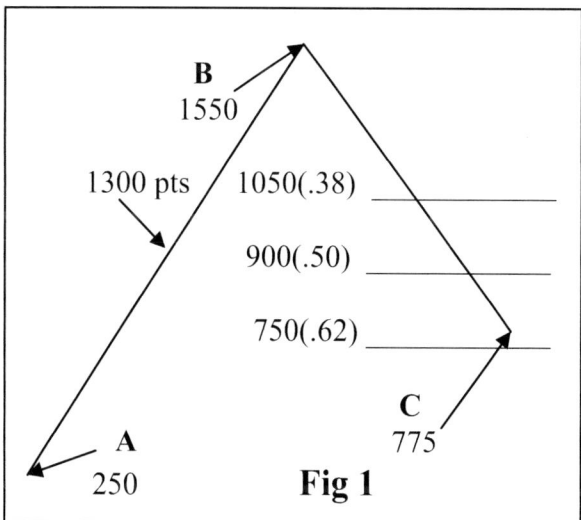

B
1550

1300 pts   1050(.38) _____

900(.50) _____

750(.62) _____

C
775

A
250   **Fig 1**

So for this example the retracement levels will be 1050 (.38), 900 (.50) or 750 (.62) (slight rounding).

Which retracement % are we going to go to is the question? Well, let's say that if we pass one fib % level then we should go to the next.

Let's say that we go through 1050 (.38) and then through 900 (.50) and stop just shy of 750 (.62) at the 775 round number and now form a new low point C. (Fig 1)

Don't we now have a leg down that according to Fib should get a retracement, rest or reaction leg back up to a .38, .50 or .62 level?… yes.

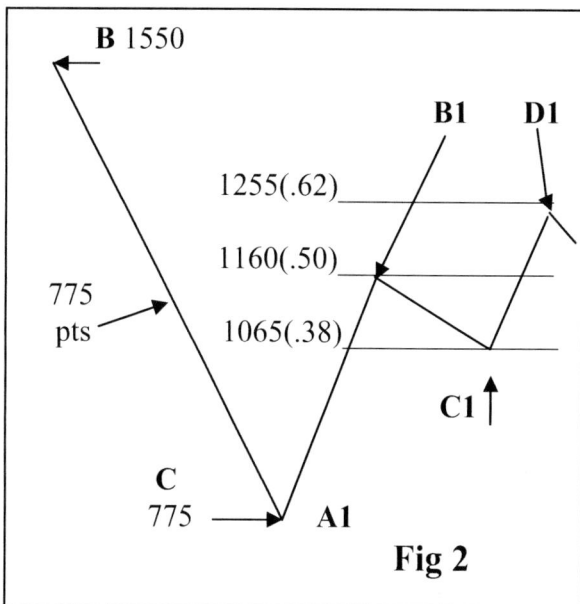

Fig 2

Those levels would be 1065 (.38), 1160 (.50) and 1255 (.62). (Fig 2)

Let's say for our example we stop at the 1160 (.50) B1 and then we pull back to the 1065 (.38) C1 level, then move up to the 1245 D1 area.

There is a very good reason for using such bizaar numbers for my example.

Nice round numbers would have been easier is what you must be thinking. Here is the explanation. Fig 1 and Fig 2 are both the S&P500 Index.

What you are looking at is the S&P 500 Index for the last 17 years!

The trading history of the S&P 500 Index followed the Fib rules for the last 17 years!

Remember we have decided to trade the Major Market Indexes via the Eminis Index Futures Contract. The S&P500 Emini mirrors or shadows the S&P Index! The Eminis basically are the S&P 500 Index, since they mirror or shadow it!

Greg Dalessandri

The Eminis mirror the index and move to Fibs or "God's Rhythm" all day every day down to the smallest time frames!

Point A was the low after the market crash in October 1987. Point B is the high in Jan 2000. Point C is the low in 2002. (Fig 1)

The markets leg up after the Oct 1987 crash was the beginning or the bottom of a 12-year run, which was a 1300-point move. The reaction or rest move back to 775 point C in 2002 was within 25 points of the .62 retracement of that 1300-point Leg Up!

Then the retracement leg up from the 775-point B-C leg down was right to the point B1 1160 (.50). If you will notice since the high of 2000 and the low of 2002 and the initial reaction leg back up to point B1 1160 (.50) retracement, we have been stuck in what I call a Fib Pinch. We are bouncing between the .38 and the .62 from that High of 2000 point B and low of 2002 point C. (Fig 2)

Incidentally we had the exact same formation after 9/11. We were stuck in a FIB Pinch after that horrible event for months. Fibs worked even after that horrific attack. (Fig 3)

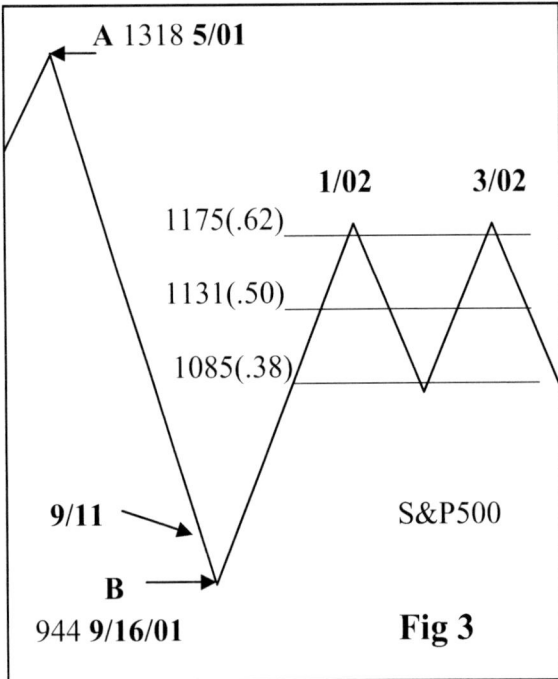

A 1318 **5/01**

1/02   **3/02**

1175(.62)

1131(.50)

1085(.38)

9/11   S&P500

B

944 **9/16/01**   **Fig 3**

These formations as I have stated, are duplicated over and over again. During a typical trading day we recognize and trade these same formations using the smallest of time frames and therefore can capture our "Manna of the Day" of 10-20 points a day in a few hours!

This is how remarkable Fibs are at predicting the markets movements!

Given the time, space, and chart detail, which would literally be countless volumes I could show you how this rhythm repeats itself on every time frame for indexes, and individual stocks to the point that it is simply phenomenal and beyond words!

Lets use Fig 3 as an example, if instead of it being a weekly chart showing us the price movement of a year, it is a one minute chart. So the starting point or Point "A" is where we started for the day when

the NYSE opens at 9:30 am EST. This
type of chart is what we would see in a
typical 20- 30-minute period of time. Of
course the amount of movement or the
length of the legs would be smaller than
our example chart, but would give us the
formations we would be looking for to
capture our 'Manna for the Day". You see
we trade these exact same formations
every single day…over and over again!

We have learned to recognize them with
all their inherent nuances and dynamics as
the market is trading real time! What does
all this result in? "Traders for the Master"
seizing the wealth of the world for the
purpose of spreading the gospel and doing
good works!

When you combine the power and
simplicity of "God's Rhythm" with
"Leveraged Instruments", as we discussed
in the last chapter, while trading with the
"Cash Flow" model and the account sizes
below, this is the result:

$2,500 x 20 pts a day = $24,000 a year
$5,000 x 20 pts a day= $48,000 a year
$15,000 x 20 pts a day=$288,000 a year
$30,000 x 20 pts a day= $576,000 a year
$60,000 x 20 pts a day= $1,152,000 a year

Or by using the "Compounding" model example from the last chapter: (page 64)

$10,000 x 20 pts a day = $4 Million in ONE YEAR!

And on, And on!

Are you starting to see the power of what we are doing?

It is very exciting to see the students of TradingFaith becoming accomplished "Traders for the Master" They are learning to recognize "God's Rhythm" while trading the Eminis and realizing the reality of "Practical Prosperity".

They are in real world training to receive the Finances for the purpose of Spreading the Gospel and to Do Good Works! What an exciting time we are living in!

It is truly God's hand at work!

God spoke and wove this Rhythm into creation, we as his followers and believers who are commissioned to Spread the Gospel are now learning specifically how to apply this revelation.

Coupled with "New Technology", and Leveraged Instruments" we can now trade to seize the wealth of the world!

If we understand that God wants us to prosper for the purpose of Spreading the Gospel. That we now have unlimited fields facilitated by New Technology, high-speed Internet connections and Direct Access Brokers. That we also now have the ability through the revelation of Leveraged stable Emini Market Index Futures Contracts to trade. And, that there is "God's Rhythm" that shows us "How To Trade" with an incredible degree of understanding and predictability to achieve our "Manna for the Day". Then there is only one additional thing to consider…

HOW DOES A BELIEVER RECEIVE THE NECESSARY TRAINING/ MENTORING TO BECOME A SUCCESFUL ACCOMPLISHED "TRADER FOR THE MASTER"?

Besides our primary Fib trading tool, there are additional tools that we use to help us to identify our trades. We also use Multiple Time Frames, Moving Averages, Candlesticks, Formations etc.

How does a believer called to this financial outpouring walk in understanding of how to use all of these tools? How long does it take to learn and really become accomplished and successful? Where does a believer go to receive training and mentoring for this? How does a believer become a "Trader for the Master"?

Learning to use these tools as the dynamics of the markets are constantly moving and changing is the next critical step to walking in "Practical Prosperity" and what I am committed too!

The next chapter is dedicated to the final critical precept and building block.

In the next chapter we will discuss how the believer called to this financial outpouring can get the training/ mentoring necessary to become a "Trader for the Master". Hang on, as we now will discuss ...

"Training for God's Covenant People"

Greg Dalessandri

Chapter 5

Training for God's Covenant People

The last building block to consider for walking in "Practical Prosperity" is to look seriously at the training/ mentoring a believer would require to become a "Trader for the Master"

It was my goal after receiving the revelations of "Leveraged Instruments", and "God's Rhythm" to help believers that sought my help to walk in these revelations. At first the training was a simple meeting of a few friends that had the same dream that I did. To be a Financial Blessing, to Fund God's Work, and to Spread the Gospel. They all had the desire to spend more time with their families and also to spend more time involved in ministry. Could the extra funds allow their wives to stay home with their children? All of this was part of the original vision.

God of course had a much bigger vision, and like the skin of an onion pulled back each layer at the perfect time for me to see what he wanted to do.

In Chapter 1, I discussed my promise to God that I would be willing to train those that he would send to me. He met me every step along my journey and at his perfect timing taught me all the things I needed to know. I watched traders fail all around me. But God was my refuge and my strength. As I committed my ways to him he was directing my paths. As he taught me the truths of "Leveraged Instruments" and "God's Rhythm", I started to realize that anyone in the Body of Christ with a calling to financial giving could do this. I started to realize that my promise might mean more then just a few of my friends.

In the beginning, as my friends asked for my help, training, direction and responded to the power of "God's Rhythm", our training meetings were held at a restaurant where I would draw out the concepts that we have been discussing on a little white board…. That was about to change!

My heart was that we should have a Live Trading Room, where we could all communicate as the market was opening. We could all be looking at the same screens in our own respective homes, and I could point out God's Rhythm, with this idea, TradingFaith.com was born.

After the creation of the site in the summer of 2004, with the Live Trading Room, I started to see that the students needed more.

God started to stir in me the ideas of what the students needed. The task seemed enormous at the time. I was thinking back to when I first started trading in 1999 and what I needed. Not necessarily what I thought I needed at the time, but what I now know I needed. I knew I could use this insight to develop the training for the new students.

How can I capture the entire trading strategy and deliver it in a way that someone could really learn it? Of course, with the main focus being to dedicate the training and site to the Body of Christ.

I would first need to create a DVD Training Video and offer Live Mentoring Classes. The DVD's would need to cover all the theory of God's Rhythm as well as the markets and additional information concerning trading strategies. Designed so the student can watch it repeatedly and create a firm foundation. The Mentoring Classes would have to include both Video and Audio, and be available Live over the Internet so anyone, anywhere can attend. With these classes I could give personalized live mentoring, explaining every nuance of the trading system.

I could show how and where the trade setups are as the dynamics of the market is actually changing. What if then, I could record the classes and archive them to the site so the students could watch them over and over? I had used this type of technology to hold Online Classes in previous jobs, and this type of technology was very expensive. Expensive or not, this is what the students would need.

With this level of mentoring the students can watch the charts unfold, with live guidance, learning how God's Rhythm" works, in detail, as the market is constantly moving and changing its dynamics.

With this level of training/ mentoring
I could truly raise up
"Traders for the Master"!

I would also need to be able to deliver this training repeatedly and over a long enough period of time that it really sinks in! That's what I need to create! God Help!

For the student to succeed, I also needed to consider in the training process their relationship with a Broker. This was a big part of my beginnings, and I realized that the students would need help concerning both the selection and setup of their accounts with the Broker as well as guidance with the software that they will be using to display the charts, and execute their orders. This is a critical piece.

Additionally, if the students could all be watching the charts and executing trades on the same software platform, then they simply would learn faster. So with this in mind, I needed to establish a relationship with a first class Futures Broker that offered the software that has the features and execution speed that we require. Fortunately, the broker and software that I had been using for over four years was a great choice. So this relationship was already in place. I had chosen TerraNova, L.L.C., [1] (TN) as my Direct Access Broker. They are one of the leading Futures Brokers in the country. They have standardized on the Townsend Analytics, Ltd. trading software platform called RealTick® [2](RT).

The software has all the features that the trader requires. TN also has a fully staffed Customer Support and Trading Desk to help with any type of problem that can arise with the trader's account, the software, and specific trades. They offer free on-line software tutorials and software training classes, which allows TradingFaith to focus on training the trading strategy. TN also offers full Demo and Simulator modes so that the ttraders can practice trading on fake money during their learning startup phase. TN has also facilitated a dedicated Representative to TradingFaith's students.

1 TerraNova, L.L.C., member NASD, NFA, SIPC, PCX, & ISE.
2 RealTick is a registered trademark of Townsend Analytics Ltd

His name is Tim Gentry. You can contact Tim at 800-525-1670 to discuss getting started and setting up a futures account.

I had a dream early on in the site's development. In this dream I handed God a rusty, held together with wire, falling apart, unsafe tricycle, and said "here I made this for your children". The dream then changed, and in this new scene I handed him a beautiful, polished, safe, tricycle and said "here I made this for your children".

With God's grace, I have set out to create a Christian Based Training Organization for the express purpose of training and developing "Traders for the Master". It had to be spectacular, and beyond reproach. I am someday going to stand before God and say "I created this for your children"!

TradingFaith.com was created with this dream in mind. Secular training organizations are offering far less and charging much more.

What I am training and offering is also a completely different strategy than the secular organizations. The strategy that I am teaching is based on five distinct different factors:

- Trading the Major Market Indexes
- Trading the Major Markets via the Eminis "leveraged Instruments"
- Trading thc Eminis using 'God's Rhythm" including Reverse Fibs, Fib Pinch and Dance, Transitions, Head Fakes, Double Pump retracements & Bull/Bear traps
- Trading using a "Multiple Time Frame" strategy
- And, lastly the development of a training/ mentoring program fit for "God's Covenant People" where the main focus is the collection of funds for the pure purpose of Spreading the Gospel and doing Good Works

Bundling these things together is exclusive to TradingFaith, especially when you consider that we are giving:

God the Credit, and all for the Sole Purpose of Fulfilling His Will!

Let's walk through what a mentoring student of TradingFaith receives and God has helped me to create so you can further understand.

Once the students get discussions with Tim from TN underway, and sign up as a student with TradingFaith, they will receive Demo software to play with. This software allows the student to "play trade"… a very powerful tool! They can download pre-configured screen page setups from TradingFaith.com so they will be looking at the same layouts, charts, and information that the other students and traders in TradingFaith are watching. During this time the student also receives a three-hour DVD training video. It is the foundational starting point and has all the theory on it that makes the trading strategy work. It was designed so the student can watch the theory over and over, and start to understand how to capture their "Manna for the Day" There is no substitute for repetition and time (experience). Mentoring students rave about the content on these DVD's, saying that even after attending the live mentoring classes and then going back to review them there is something new that they see.

The student each morning then starts attending the Live Trading Room. The NYSE opens at 9:30 EST. All the traders/students start coming in around that time, and I and some of the other more advanced students start pointing out God's Rhythm, the Fibs, setups, entries, etc...

Live, as the Trades are Occurring.

The Live Trading Room is text based and every time someone types something into the room a sound can be heard on your computers speakers so you can be alerted, and read and follow the comments in the room.

The new students are asking questions as the Room is designed for interaction and refining the trader's skills. This goes on for a couple of hours or so, while everyone is going for their "Manna for the Day" goal. Once a week (currently Friday) instead of a text based trading room, we hold what we call a Live Trading Room. In the Live Trading Room, all of us are on a phone conference call and at the same time all the students can see my screens or charts from my computer on their computers. Where ever they happen to be geographically located. As the market is moving and while we are all watching my screens, we are discussing all the dynamics of the trading strategies! It is basically like all of us sitting in my office watching live as the markets unfold.

I then break for my Monday through Friday Radio Show TradingFaith at 11:00 EST on www.CFRN.net (Christian Financial Radio Network) where I discuss the markets movements for that day etc.

The students can tune in to help with their understanding of the day, and how God's Rhythm is working. I also post the recorded copy of the Radio Show interview along with my Live charts on the www.TradingFaith.com site.

At the end of the day I post the Nightly "Stock Market Video Recap" for the students review. This is a nightly VIDEO review of what the market did for the day, as well as why and where it is trying to go next. In this Recap, I walk them visually through the charts using video. They simply sit back watch and listen. I focus on the Bird's Eye View and bring it down to a tighter intraday view. On the Friday edition, I also discuss the market from the bigger Bird's Eye View as a weekly review perspective.

This Nightly Stock Market VIDEO Recap is the first of it's kind. It was birthed from a typed nightly newsletter that I was doing, and the Lord revealed to me one day, the entire idea of creating it using **Video**!

You can find an example under the "Free Samples" link on TradingFaith.com.

So while watching the DVD's repeatedly, the student is in the Live Trading Room every day getting live input on actual trades as they are forming. They are looking at the same pre-configured page setup screens that we are all looking at, while on a demo or simulator able to place and practice trades. They can then listen to the TradingFaith radio segment live (or the posted recorded version) to further add a foundation to what they just witnessed in the markets. And then every night also receives a Video Recap of what the market did and what it is going to try to do next.

There is more, I also currently offer Live Online Mentoring Classes on Tuesday and Thursday evenings. In these two live online classes I walk the students through the charts and discuss all the nuances, Fib entries, exits, and every possible aspect of God's Rhythm and trading. Both the Video and Audio is live.

The students in the classes are looking at my screens… remotely. They are literally watching my charts on their computers live, wherever geographically they happen to be. I move the charts, use pointers and draw lines etc as all the students are watching! The audio discussion is on a live phone conference call as well, so the students and I can interact, everyone can hear everyone. This makes for some fun banter and dialogue! We use the same technology format for these classes that we use in our Friday Morning Live Trading Room.

The Tuesday Market Overview Class is dedicated to a Bigger Picture Bird's Eye View of the market, and usually lasts for one hour. The Thursday Class is a Personal Mentoring Class and dedicated to getting into and learning all the nuances of integrating and managing multiple time frames, recognizing all the entries, exits etc. This class usually lasts at least two hours in length.

The market's dynamics are constantly moving and changing, in these classes we can slow down the movement to our pace and discuss every aspect of the trading strategy. Any student with a computer, high-speed Internet connection and phone can attend these classes!

The technology to hold these classes is expensive and TN sponsors these mentoring classes. They are as dedicated as I am to the success of the traders!

These classes are very powerful and the ingredient and place where the students really learn the techniques required to become an accomplished "Trader for the Master".

You can also find examples of these classes under the "Free Samples" link on TradingFaith.com

In October 2004, I discovered the technology to record these classes. The mentoring students can not only attend these live classes, but also can go on to the TradingFaith site and REVIEW and WATCH the ARCHIVED CLASSES! Currently, (May 2006) there are over 300 hours of classes recorded and archived on the site for the mentoring students to review! This includes the Friday Morning Live Trading Room as well!

So quick review; during the time the students receive and are repeatedly watching the 3-hour DVD training video where the complete theory of the trading system and strategies are discussed, they are accessing the daily Live Trading Room. In the Trading Room the dynamics of God's Rhythm, setups and trades are pointed out Live, as they are occurring "real time". Then the students can tune in to hear me live discuss the days markets movement on the TradingFaith radio show on CFRN.net. Then at the end of each trading day the students also receive the nightly Stock Market Video Recap so they can sit back and watch me walk them through what happened that day and why, as further confirmation to the comments that were in the Live Trading Room and the TradingFaith radio show that morning. Also, on Tuesday and Thursday evenings they attend the Live Online Mentoring Classes. And on Friday the students attend the Live Friday Morning Trading Room Class. After attending the live classes the students can then review any of the Archived Mentoring and Live Trading Room Classes that have been posted on the TradingFaith site, at their leisure!

It is with the DVD's and the nightly Video Recaps and especially the Live Mentoring Classes that I really get into teaching the system walking through every nuance of God's Rhythm, dynamics and trade setups. It is then in the Live Trading Room that the student learns to Practice what they are learning while the trades are occurring Live.

Basically the students are inundated with training/ mentoring!

The students are receiving a minimum of 15 hours of live instruction every week! Along with access to the 3 hour DVD training video and Access to the 300+ hours (currently May 06) of Archived Mentoring and Live Trading Room Classes

Now here is the question, how long does the student receive this level of training/ mentoring?

The students receive everything that I discussed above for an entire 2 ½ months or 10 weeks!

The objective is to bring the student to the level of being accomplished and successful. Why 2½ months, because after considering where I was at my beginnings this was the minimum amount of training/ mentoring that a student would require to truly become a "Trader for the Master"!

It was also one of my goals with developing TradingFaith to create a learning environment that would hopefully cut down on the amount of time and finances (compared to my journey) that a student would have to spend to become a "Trader for the Master". Of course, understanding that every student would have a different learning curve and journey due to their individual factors.

After prayer and consulting with the covering pastors that I have in place over TradingFaith, the amount to be charged for this mentoring has currently been set at;

$2,000!

And, every student that finishes the 2½ month, 10 week mentoring program can continue receiving everything described above for as long as they choose, for the monthly subscription fee of $75.

In this level of membership the students can also attend another Class designed especially for them. This Live Continued Education Class is dedicated to just the students that have completed the 2½ month, 10 week mentoring program.

In this class we expand on the trading strategies and help the students fine-tune their trading skills and their vision as they pursue their goal of becoming an established, successful "Trader for the Master".

The quantity and quality of this training is why I have titled it:

"Training for God's Covenant People"!

I currently offer a **FREE TRIAL** period on TradingFaith. During this **FREE** Trial period the student can access the Live Trading Room, receive the nightly Stock Market Video Recaps and join the Tuesday night Live Market Overview Mentoring Class. After the **FREE** Trial period, for those that aren't quite ready to step into the full 2½ month Mentoring Program that I have been describing, they can choose to sign up for an Entry Level membership and continue to receive everything (and more) that they received with their **FREE** Trial for the current set monthly cost of $75.

I have attempted to create and offer a number of different membership levels of training available to meet the diverse needs of the students that would like to say "Yes", to this call.

The full detailed descriptions of the different levels of memberships available on TradingFaith can be found under the "Membership" link on the home page of www.TradingFaith.com.

With God's help the original vision that I had for the training of the Body of Christ has been created! It is robust, and contains the visual training tools and repetition that is needed to bring the student to full maturity as an accomplished "Trader for the Master"! I can truly stand before God and say, "by your grace Father, I have made this for your children"!

The testimonial section of the website is growing. The student's are speaking out loudly in their comments concerning their journey; you can truly see God's hand at work! Not only am I seeing the financial victory, where the traders are achieving their "Manna for the Day" goals,

But, I am also witnessing relationships being restored as well. Fathers and Sons, Sisters, Brothers, Mothers and Sons, as they pursue the common goal of learning to become "Traders for the Master".

What are some of the characteristics and attitudes that I have recognized that lead to a person becoming a successful "Trader for the Master"?

The student needs a minimum commitment of 3-6 months, and possibly 6-12 months to the learning process and journey. They should be prepared, and diligently commit themselves to this amount of time. The more time the student can spend utilizing the services offered by TradingFaith, including the live and archived classes, will prove beneficial. Also, a commitment to spending time watching the live screens/ charts, what we call "screen time" is important. The student needs to also embrace, that during the natural learning process and journey, they will probably loose money, or have "drawdown" in their account. All students need to understand that trading is risky and TradingFaith is not making any specific recommendation to buy or sell, and that the efforts of TradingFaith is to only train the student concerning the trading strategy.

The student needs to take full responsibility for their trading decisions and resist the impulse to become frustrated, find blame, and compare themselves to the other students during their training journey.

Those called to the ministry of giving, and called to be a financial blessing, to fund the Spreading of the Gospel and to do Good Works. Those called to this form of financial outpouring. Each student needs to commit to prayer and hearing God's voice and direction concerning the specific vision that God would have them to do.

Those with some familiarization with getting around a computer, Those with patience, that can manage their emotions and have the ability to focus, while stepping back and see the bigger picture without being over analytical.

God is Truly Doing Great Things!

Is God Calling You?

Revelation 11:15 says "The kingdoms of this world are become the kingdoms of our Lord and of his Christ" (KJ). Is this passage speaking of this age? I don't think I would get much debate that the financial markets are a "kingdom of this world". Is it the time to make it the "Kingdom of our Lord and of his Christ"?

For the first time in history everything to facilitate this financial outpouring is in place!

Greg Dalessandri

TradingFaith is privileged to currently be mentoring students from every walk of life; Pastors, Chaplains, Worship Leaders, Businessmen, Hedge Fund Managers, Certified Financial Planners, CPA's, Programmers, Contractors, Managers, Realtors, Engineers, Doctors, Husbands & Wife teams, Homemakers, and Retirees.

TradingFaith is also currently working with National Church Associations, Bible Colleges, Men's Rehabilitation Ministries and more.

Thank you for spending this time with me and I look forward to seeing you at TradingFaith.com if God is speaking to your spirit to become involved with this financial outpouring.

Greg Dalessandri

Here are a few comments from the students of TradingFaith.com

---

Over the last several years I have read book after book and been to seminars of all types, but I have not been so successful and blessed since I got under your mentorship.
Thanks Greg,
Arizona

I started "toying" with futures in January and lost some money. It was about that time that I felt that there was more to learn and I signed up for Greg's program at TradingFaith. I can honestly say that it has made all the difference. I equate my previous training as my "undergraduate" degree in trading, but Greg's training has propelled me to the "Masters/Ph.D" level. He has a very keen ability to relay this information in a clear and simple way that anyone can understand. Also, the technology that he uses to conduct his classes is amazing!! All of the classes, mentoring and nightly recaps are done with live video that you sit back at your desk and watch over your computer. All the while, you're live on the phone in real-time watching Greg's actual trading screens as he walks thru the charts tick by tick. He shows and explains every setup, entry, exit, stop and every scenario in between. The DVD's are an excellent start to grasp the concepts of the system, but the mentoring is where it all comes together and you get proficient at application. It's one thing to know the system, but quite another to be able to actually do it. The mentoring will get you there. I'm convinced it is how the markets really work. I highly recommend Greg's program at TradingFaith.

Arizona

Greg

Your "lecturing" to me yesterday really helped me to relax and I made some good (robotic!) trades today. 30 points in 4 trades. That's good for me, but more importantly, my mindset was "mellow"--- that was really really awesome!!!!!!!.... THANKS!!!!!!!!!!!!.....

Arizona

Hey Greg,

Just wanted to let you know that things are going great! I'm finally starting see the big picture, and with that my trading has drastically improved. There's such an interesting learning curve, for me anyway, with this system. About two weeks into the training, after watching the DVDs and attending a couple of classes, I was sure that I had it figured out. Close above the 5, punch through the 50, retracement, bla, bla, bla. It sounds so easy!!! Well, after losing about a trillion dollars on the simulator in the first month I realized I had some more learning to do. I re-watched the DVDs a couple of times, memorized the major numbers on the S & P, and really tried to focus on integrating all of the time frames into each trade. Now I'm getting 20 points more often than not, and only getting better. My trading this morning was the incentive for this email. 20 points in 40 minutes, and 2 trades. Not bad for someone who had never made a single trade before January (2 months ago).

Thanks and keep up the good work

Oregon

---

20 Points a day with only 1 hour to trade...thanks for everything Greg

Arizona

Your system is well taught, easy to learn, and a bright guy or gal can get going relatively quickly. the difference is the mentoring...sets yours apart.

Florida

Greg

To give credit where credit is due I would have to say it is because of your teaching acumen. I really appreciate all you have done for me and your faithfulness to continue to show others the way to victory in this area of life.

Minnesota

Greg

As I'm packing away my laptop for Hawaii, I was just thinking about how I would never be going if it weren't for your mentoring!
My thanks to you and, I promise that at our first dinner, my boys and I will raise a glass in your honor!!

Arizona

I thought the mentoring was awesome! It was so powerful seeing it all unfold right on the screen. I think the new way of doing the nightly newsletter is terrific.

Wisconsin

Greg

Just got a chance last night to review your Video Recaps. They are truly unique. Your commentary is interesting and your presentation superb. I really enjoyed all the animation in your voice from time to time, making the whole experience entertaining. Your daily analysis provided a new perspective to the daily market moves.

Arizona

Greg, I really enjoyed our conversation today. I have been looking for a long time for people who want to help others for little or no gain to themselves. Since my separation I feel I've been abandoned by just about everyone I know including my rabbi. This is very refreshing for me at this time.

North Carolina

I have been getting my points overnight and by trading the bigger picture. Thanks for all your hard work, you are very tenacious and loyal. I am grateful for what

God has put into your heart. You have been a true and faithful servant giving huge quantities of time and care into many of us out of your loyalty to a promise made to God.

Arizona

Greg,

The recaps are awesome and truly give the big picture of what is happening behind the market. Because it truly is a battle between the buyers and sellers. You see the picture clearly and the fibs makes sense of it all

Texas

Greg Dalessandri

About The Author

Greg Dalessandri spent 12 years in the software industry, where he was responsible for launching 2 successful start-up companies. He has also served as a youth pastor, and worship leader. Since 1999 he has been a full time trader. He has become a nationally recognized Index Futures Trader, utilizing and refining God's Rhythm, a unique trading strategy that foresees the Markets price action with incredible predictability.

You can hear Greg on the TradingFaith Radio Show, broadcast on Christian Financial Radio Network (www.cfrn.net) Monday – Friday at 11:00 EST. He has been featured in and is a contributing writer for <u>Active Trader Magazine</u>. He is the founder of the J1MLP Trading System, and www.TradingFaith.com. He has served as a Guest/Seminar speaker for numerous Investment Clubs and Investors Business Daily Groups.

Through www.TradingFaith.com he is currently mentoring students to become "Traders for the Master", for the specific purpose of raising finances to further God's Kingdom from all walks of Life, including: Pastors, Chaplains, Worship Leaders, Hedge Fund Managers, Doctors, Engineers, CPA's, Business Owners, Contractors, Realtors, Professional Traders, Husband & Wife teams, Homemakers & Retirees.